GROOM

BRIDE

A Bridal Blessing

BLUE LANTERN BOOKS

MCMXCIX

A Bridal Blessing

WELLERAN POLTARNEES

COPYRIGHT © 1997 BLUE LANTERN STUDIO. ALL RIGHTS RESERVED.
THIRD PRINTING. PRINTED IN HONG KONG.

ISBN 1-883211-11-5

BLUE LANTERN BOOKS
PO BOX 4399   SEATTLE, WASHINGTON 98104
800.354.0400

I send you
this blessing.
It embodies
my wishes
for this,
the time of
your wedding,
and
for all the
times to come.

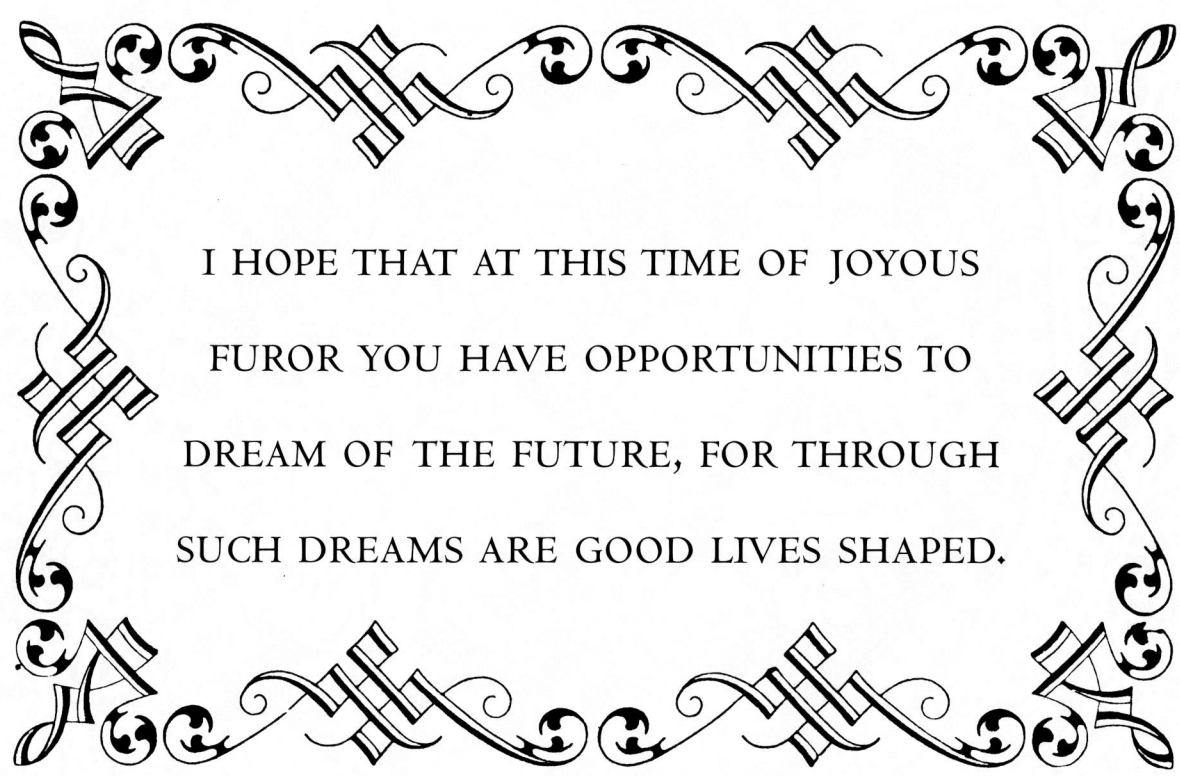

I HOPE THAT AT THIS TIME OF JOYOUS FUROR YOU HAVE OPPORTUNITIES TO DREAM OF THE FUTURE, FOR THROUGH SUCH DREAMS ARE GOOD LIVES SHAPED.

I BLESS THE FRIENDS WHO SURROUND YOU,

AND HOPE THAT THEIR SUSTAINING

LOVE WILL GIVE STRENGTH TO

YOUR BLOSSOMING.

MAY YOU, ON THE MORNING OF YOUR

WEDDING, WAKE IN SURETY AND PEACE,

AND MAY YOU FIND, DURING THIS BUSY

DAY, A FEW MOMENTS FOR SOLITUDE AND

REFLECTION.

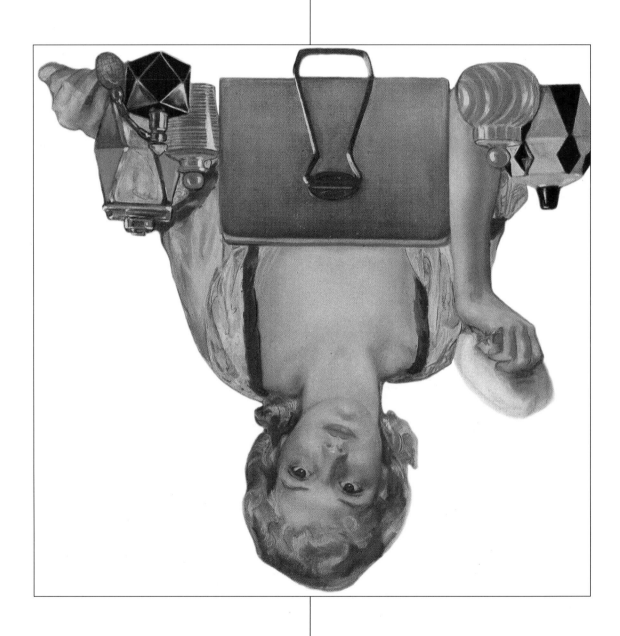

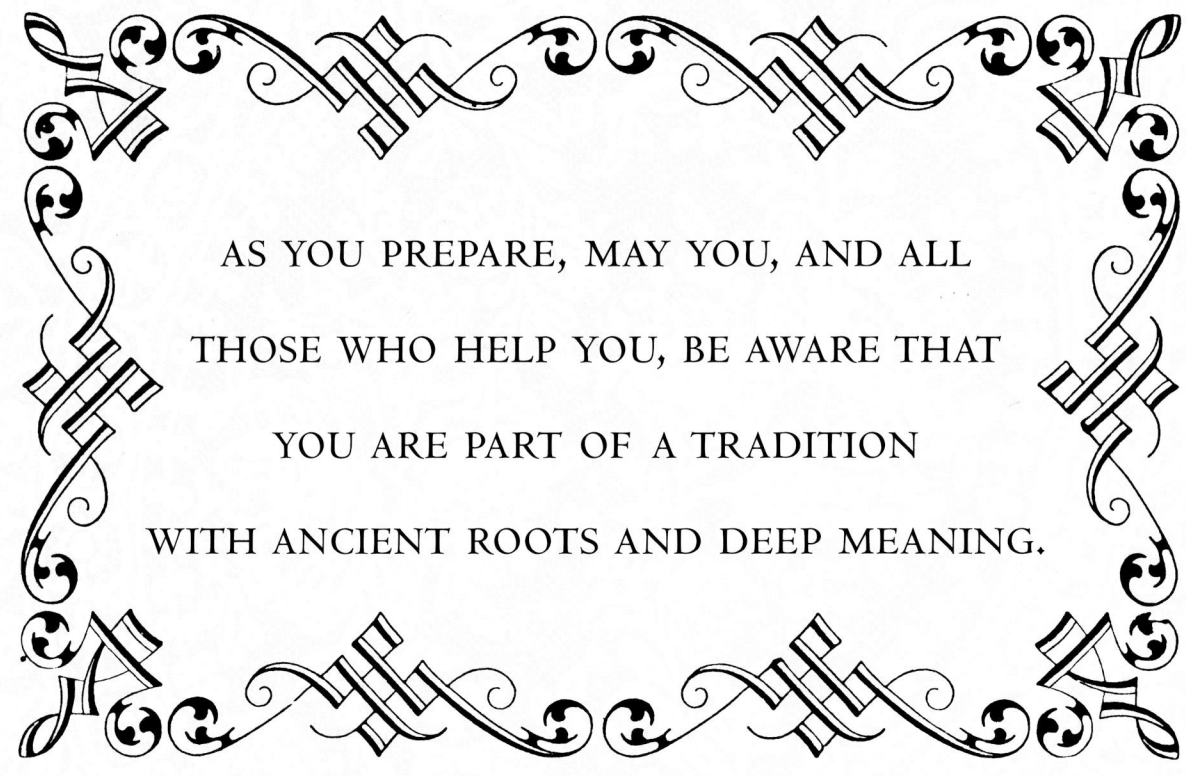

AS YOU PREPARE, MAY YOU, AND ALL

THOSE WHO HELP YOU, BE AWARE THAT

YOU ARE PART OF A TRADITION

WITH ANCIENT ROOTS AND DEEP MEANING.

LET THERE BE, "SOMETHING OLD,

SOMETHING NEW, SOMETHING

BORROWED, SOMETHING BLUE."

THIS IS A TIME OF FLOWERS. MAY EACH OF

THEM GIVE TO YOU NOT ONLY ITS BEAUTY

AND FRAGRANCE, BUT ALSO THE SYMBOLIC

MEANING THAT HUMAN EXPERIENCE HAS

ADDED TO THEM.

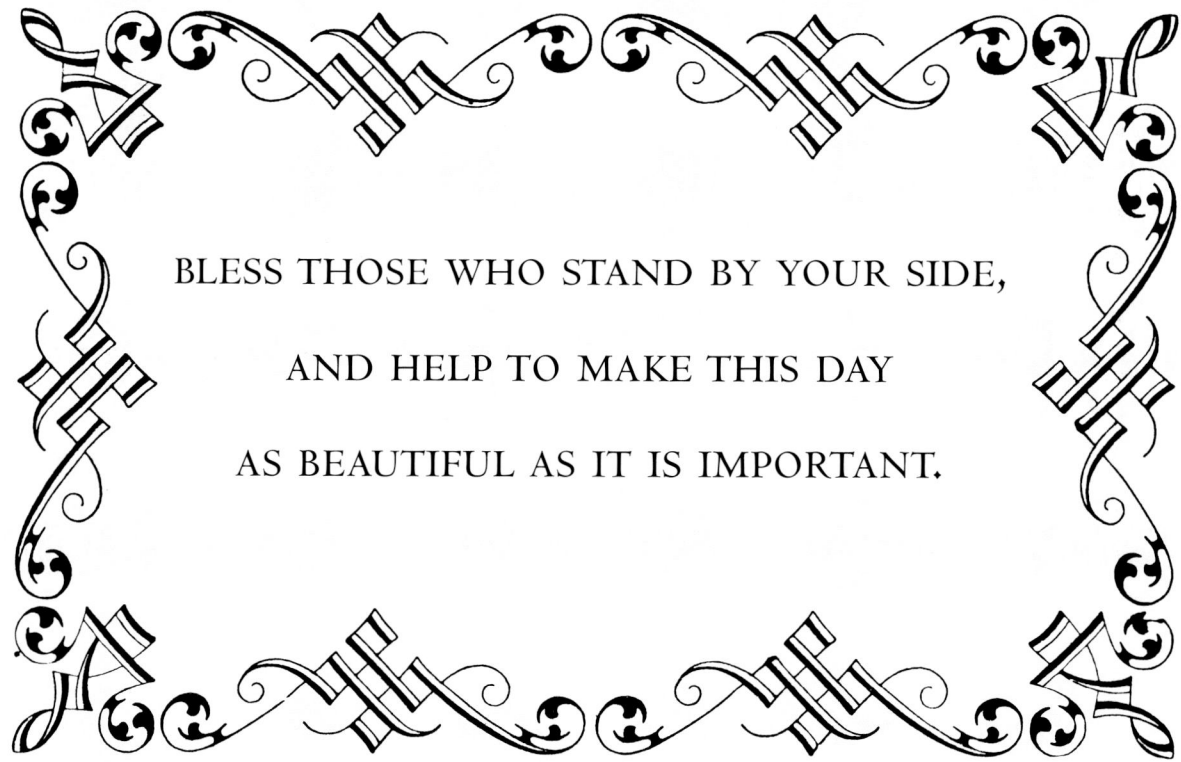

BLESS THOSE WHO STAND BY YOUR SIDE,

AND HELP TO MAKE THIS DAY

AS BEAUTIFUL AS IT IS IMPORTANT.

BLESSED BE THE RING YOU WEAR, A

UNIVERSAL SYMBOL OF CONTINUITY

AND WHOLENESS — SIMPLE,

PERFECT, INEVITABLE.

MAY IT BE GIVEN TO YOU, AND TO THE

BRIDEGROOM, TO SEE YOURSELVES AS PART OF

A GREAT STREAM OF TRADITION IN WHICH

LOVE IS GIVEN ITS RIGHTFUL AND CENTRAL

PLACE IN OUR LIVES.

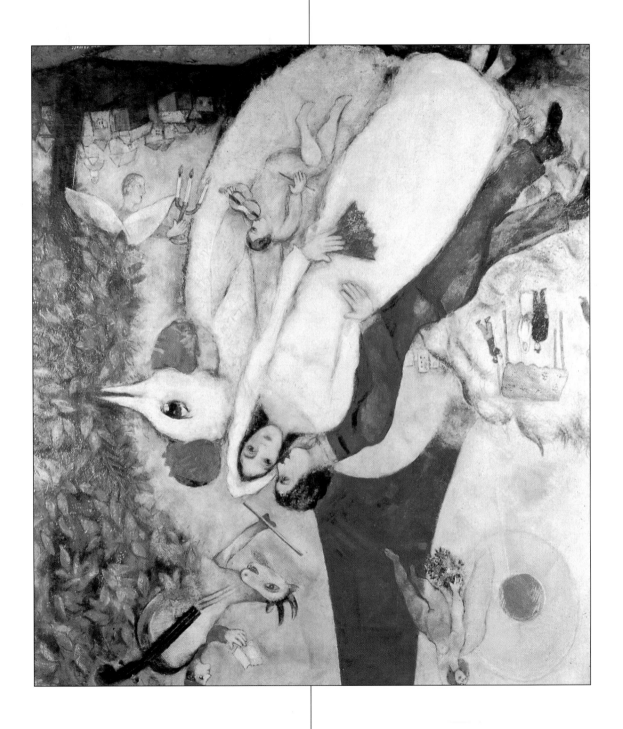

AS YOU WALK INTO THE WORLD,

LET IT BE AS MADE NEW.

I WISH FOR YOU A JOYOUS CELEBRATION, A

TOASTING, A BREAKING OF BREAD, AND

AN UNVEILING OF GIFTS; A FAREWELL TO

THE OLD, AND A WELCOMING OF THE NEW.

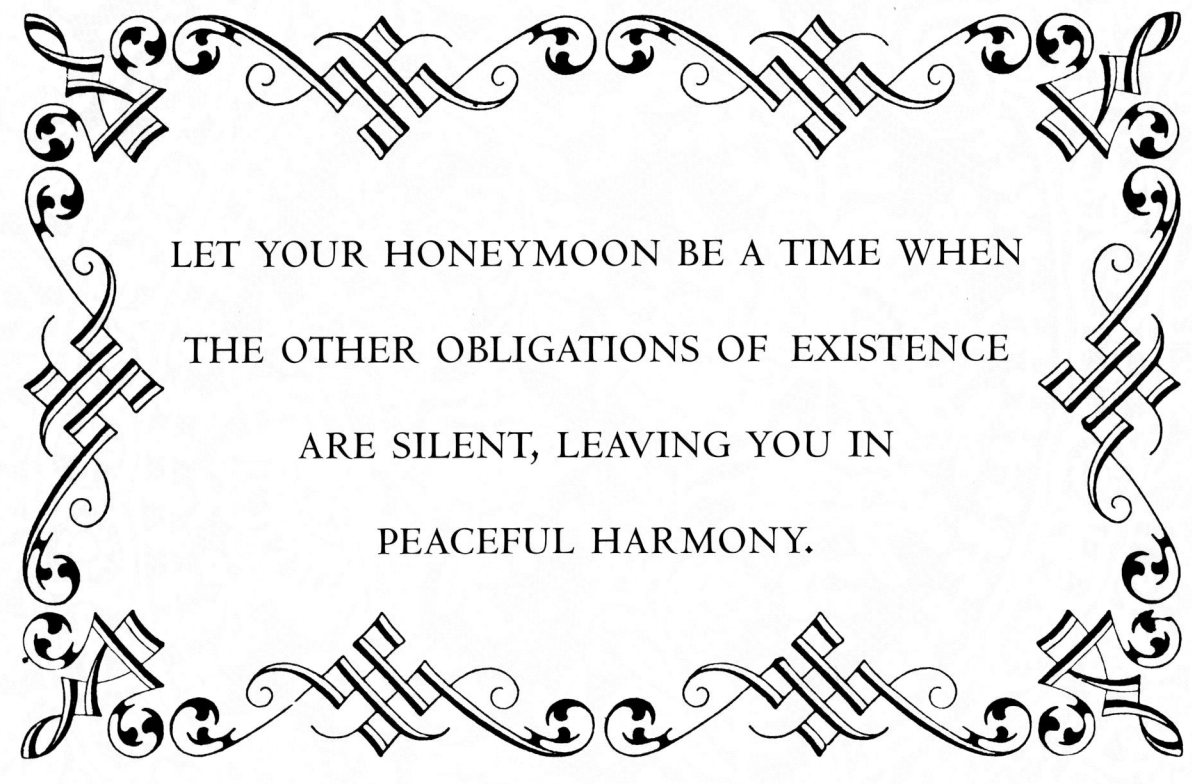

LET YOUR HONEYMOON BE A TIME WHEN

THE OTHER OBLIGATIONS OF EXISTENCE

ARE SILENT, LEAVING YOU IN

PEACEFUL HARMONY.

I BLESS YOUR FIRST HOME TOGETHER,

HOPING THAT IT BE A SUBTLY INTERTWINED

PRODUCT OF BOTH YOUR DREAMS, AND

THAT IN IT HAPPINESS MAY FLOWER.

MAY EACH OF YOU MAKE FRIENDS

OF THE OTHER'S FRIENDS, AND MAY

YOU TOGETHER FIND NEW COMRADES.

BLESS YOU INTO

THE UNKNOWABLE FUTURE.

BIBLIOGRAPHY

THIS BOOK IS TYPESET IN MONOTYPE CENTAUR.

BOOK & COVER DESIGN BY SACHEVERELL & SANDRA DARLING AT BLUE LANTERN STUDIO.

PRINTED & BOUND IN HONG KONG BY SOUTH SEAS INTERNATIONAL PRESS.